How Not to Get Rich

By the same author

The Meadowlands
A Whale Hunt
Rats

How Not to Get Rich

Or Why Being Bad Off Isn't So Bad

Robert Sullivan

Illustrations by Scott Menchin

BLOOMSBURY

10/05

Copyright © 2005 by Robert Sullivan

Published by Bloomsbury Publishing, New York and London
Distributed to the trade by Holtzbrinck Publishers

All papers used by Bloomsbury Publishing are natural,
recyclable products made from wood grown in well-managed
forests. The manufacturing processes conform to the
environmental regulations of the country of origin.

Library of Congress Cataloging-in-Publication Data

Sullivan, Robert, 1963–
    How not to get rich, or why being bad off isn't so bad /
by Robert Sullivan; illustrations by Scott Menchin.—1st U.S. ed.
        p. cm.
    Includes bibliographical references.
    ISBN 1-59691-002-X
    ISBN-13 978-1-59691-002-7
    1. Finance, Personal—Humor. 2. Self-actualization
    (Psychology)—Humor. I. Title.

HG179.S852 2005
332.024′01′0207—dc22

                                                    2005040992

First U.S. Edition 2005

1 3 5 7 9 10 8 6 4 2

Typeset by Hewer Text UK Ltd, Edinburgh
Printed in the United States of America
by Quebecor World Fairfield

For Suzanne

Contents

The life that is unexamined is not worth living.[1]

— Plato, as quoted by Phil McGraw, the television therapist who is better known as Dr. Phil, in his best-selling how-to book Life Strategies: Doing What Works, Doing What Matters

A perfect solution is being a multimillionaire. I'm perfectly happy with not being a multimillionaire.

— My wife, when once we were trying to figure out what to do in a situation where we needed money but did not have it and couldn't really expect to get it

Author's Note

THIS BOOK is intended to help you not get rich or, if you are currently not rich, to stay that way. The author makes no claims as to the effectiveness of the advice herein and in no way does he guarantee that by reading this book, the reader will stay not rich. If, for instance, the reader comes up with an idea that changes the world—gourmet coffee comes to mind, as well as Velcro and baby monitors—and in executing said idea subsequently strikes it rich, then the author cannot be held liable in any way. If, likewise, the reader has an extremely wealthy relative who passes away and leaves an enormous amount of money to the reader, then the reader should not come knocking at the author's

door. The fact is, there's not a lot the reader can do about suddenly coming into a load of money, short of giving away all that money, which, if you ask the author, is not a good idea. Don't get me wrong; I'm *for* charity and giving and so on. But giving away all of your money would be a little nutty. But we're getting off the point, which is, if you go and get rich after reading this book, it's not my fault. I certainly didn't have anything to do with it.

Foreword
By Peter DeLuvy

LET ME begin by saying that I was persuaded to write the foreword to this book on pretenses that, while not false, were at the very least unclear, and while it is true that I can't prove that the publisher or anyone else said anything about a free sports car, one has to wonder about an author who calls up a person of my stature in the professional moneymaking world at three in the morning and wrangles an agreement of any kind, much less a foreword. I should add that even after conferring with my lawyer and discovering that I was legally obliged to pen these words, I read the manuscript and attempted to dissuade the author from going ahead with publication. A question that repeatedly arose during my consultations with the author was "What's the point in all this?" It goes without saying that the author did not have much to say in his defense, if anything. True, he did sound distracted on the phone, but I wonder if the "moving men" were merely arranged for "effect." On the other hand, there seems to be a theory behind the book, though what it is I am not equipped to say. I would further posit the existence of some deep if useless understanding of precisely how *not* to get rich on the apparent author's part. At the very least, I can attest to the indisputable fact that buying it is a complete waste of time, and a complete waste of time, as we learn in the very first levels of the get-rich field, is the equivalent of a complete waste of money, as in the equation $T = M$, where T is *time* and M is *money* and L is *lunch*, which is not only not free at get-rich university but ends up being incredibly expensive because they kill you with all the little extras like monogrammed silk napkins and diamond-studded drink stirrers. Thus, it can be said that this book works. Anyway, I bought it and was immediately out $9.95. Additionally, I fell fast asleep while reading it, during which time my broker called and I missed him. I don't want to go into what the broker was calling about. I've decided just to let that go. I'm beginning to see that it may not really matter.

Peter DeLuvy is a well-known financial adviser and the author of *How to Get So Rich You Can't Even See, Two Million in Two Hours*, and *Planning to Own Your Own Planet.**

---

* Peter DeLuvy is not actually a well-known financial adviser. He's actually made up. You don't think we could get an *actual* well-known financial adviser to write a foreword to a book about how *not* to get rich, do you?

How Not to Get Rich

LARGE NUMBERS of Americans are becoming rich every day, and by rich I mean loaded, as in loaded to the gills. You could soon be one of them. On the other hand, you might not be one of them, for a number of reasons, including the odds, which are weighted heavily against you. Because while large numbers of Americans are becoming rich every day, even larger numbers of Americans are *not*. How does *not* getting rich happen? At what point in your life do you become rich or not rich? Is it fate or hard work that decides whether you go on to a life with several homes and a yacht or several overloaded credit cards and a second mortgage?[2]

As strange as it sounds, studies show that hard work is what makes a person become not rich, and by not rich I should say right off that I don't mean poor—this economic category does not include the disastrously huge number of people who not only aren't getting rich but aren't able to live on what some have called an income.[3] The not rich are the people who live in that income zone that is simultaneously above the poverty line and comfortable enough to be taunted by the possibilities of greater wealth—as in much greater, as in a beach home or in some cases a home, as in health insurance that doesn't worry you sick, as in a car that works, even in the cold.

No, this book is about the people who can publicly or privately answer yes to any of the following: Do you often buy an expensive shirt or blouse that you can't afford to have dry-cleaned? Do you subscribe to one or more glossy European interior-design magazines that feature the meticulously renovated country homes of the very well-to-do while staying on a first-name basis with the security guard at your local Salvation Army? Do you have a $500 stereo in your $400 car?[4] If you are guilty of all or any of these, then you know that eventually, there comes a time in all un-extremely wealthy people's lives when they must consider whether they have at last entered the crowded halls of the non-elite.

At some point, you may say to yourself, If so many people are not getting rich quickly, then how difficult can it be to *not* get rich anyway?[5] Well, it's *not* simple. It takes a lot of emotional effort. You may know a software million-aire or have a friend who cashed out on his biotech stocks years ago, but, as you so often realize as a member of the nonrich, that friend is not you—you're the guy who laughed when he offered to get you in "on the ground floor" of what turned out to be a very tall tower. You still have a job, and you show up every day—or phone in or log in, or however it is that you greet your employer, assuming that your employer has not yet moved his operations overseas—and, as an American, you work very hard. In fact, as an American you work more productively than just about anyone else in the world, statistically speaking, and, as we well know, you don't get rich, usually without even taking vacation. (Don't look at the footnote below, comparing vacation days taken in the United States with

vacation days taken in the rest of the world, if you are reading this on a Monday morning.)*

If you have been out of college for a few years, then you have some sense of this situation already, though perhaps you are still planning on making it big in the future. If you have been out of college for one or more decades and you are not one of the 2.2 million millionaires in America, then you are fairly certain that you will not be getting rich, even though everything you see on television suggests that it could still happen, maybe any minute. America has this tendency to tease you with glimpses of abundant prosperity. America doesn't *mean* to offend you; this is just how America works, since America has always been a place to go to try something better, something new, something that involved free land, unlimited opportunity, and often the possibility of gold.

---

* The American worker works 137 hours more than the Japanese worker every year, the equivalent of $3\frac{1}{2}$ vacation weeks more, and $12\frac{1}{2}$ vacation weeks more than the German worker. According to a survey by Expedia.com, an Internet travel company, 14 percent of Americans take no vacation time, and 30 percent of the American workers who have vacation time don't use it all. Expedia estimated that 415 million vacation days went unused in 2004, the equivalent of 1.6 million years of unused vacation, enough time to finish a jigsaw puzzle.

Everything you see on TV and in magazines in America shows Americans living a life of luxury, surrounded by all the stuff that you, the viewer, didn't know you wanted and probably don't need. You watch people maneuvering between homes and second homes and vacation homes and homes that they continue to call homes even when they are in prison for lying or fraud or insider trading, a not-so-good way to get rich, by the way.

Meanwhile, it turns out that after you accumulate a certain amount, money doesn't make you a whole lot happier. A study in Holland showed that after income exceeds $10,000, money and happiness are suddenly unrelated. A *Time* poll reported that Americans are happier making more money until they make about $50,000 a year, at which point making more money no longer makes them much happier, on account of such problems as jealousy, general anxiety, and, presumably, cell phone bills, which will get you no matter how much you make or how hard you try to keep the conversation brief.[6] Money and happiness start out like a team, like peanut butter and jelly, but end up being like peanut butter and motor oil, a tasteless, self-defeating concoction.

But that's not really the point of this treatise. The point is that you have to always stay concentrated on not getting rich—and prepare yourself emotionally. You have to stay focused on *not* being focused on becoming wealthy. In the America we live in today, people are not just born not rich. They end up working at it.

FORTUNATELY, THERE ARE SEVERAL WAYS THAT YOU can prepare yourself and your loved ones for a relatively smooth path to an unrich life. And there are, likewise, a few simple ways to maintain your un-millions-encumbered ways while not getting flustered or frustrated.

The Not Rich
and History

Don't let the past fool you: The nonrich are big players throughout history. History downplays the unwealthy, relegates them to a seemingly minor role, but the nonrich can take pride in the fact that they are part of a long and undistinguished line of not-rich people. Indeed, one can safely say that the nonrich own the past. It's true that there is no equivalent of the Fortune 500 for people who have done exceptionally well at not getting rich. Our children's history books go on for pages about the robber barons and millionaires and monopolies, only to mention in passing the strikes and marches for the need of money that consumed America at various times in its history. But the very unwealthy life was the life of millions and millions of Americans at any given moment in history—and still is, not that TV news would know how to cover such things. (A good thing about not getting rich is that, if you play it right, it is a vantage point readily conducive to compassion for the other three quarters of the world's population who are truly not rich.) It's likewise true that fame and power are most often associated with

The author has himself found these ways to be helpful and practical and nearly foolproof, if that is not an oxymoron. Please note, however, that they are not scientifically proven in any way. That kind of thing would cost a lot of money, and it's not like the author is made of money, obviously. Instead, the author has looked at his own experiences and the experiences of his closest billions-free friends and attempted to draw a few simple non-moneymaking conclusions. Samuel Butler, the Victorian writer and translator, once said that the gods are those who either have money or do not want it. Having spent his no doubt valuable time translating Homer rather than, say, patenting a new method of coal production, I feel certain that Butler is as likely as anybody to have known. Anyway, in the name of full disclosure, it should be noted, in case you haven't guessed it already, that the author is at the present time, like many of his friends, a mortal. Why else would I be writing this?

wealth accumulation, two more reasons to tout both fame and power, as if they needed any more touting.

But recall, if you will, that Gutenberg, the great medieval printer, developed movable type while enduring the medieval equivalent of creditors harassing him on the phone. Someone else *owned* his tools, and yet, of Gutenberg, Mark Twain has said, "The whole world admits unhesitatingly, and there can be no doubt about this, that Gutenberg's invention is the incomparably greatest event in the history of the world." In the case of Twain lauding Gutenberg, it was the financially unlucky pot calling the bankruptcy-prone kettle black. In fact, Mark Twain's career can be analyzed in two ways. On the one hand, there is Mark Twain, the great American author and humorist, who gave us such works as *Huckleberry Finn* and *A Connecticut Yankee in King Arthur's Court* and *The Innocents Abroad.* And then there is Mark Twain the businessman, the investor who never met a bad investment he could pass up. Do you remember the steam-powered whiskey mill? Do you recall the Kaolatype, which was an engraving process that was supposed to revolutionize printing and did not? Do you remember reading about the Vaporizer, which was just some whacked-out thing? No? That's because in all those cases, after Mark Twain invested in them, the companies that produced them went belly-up.

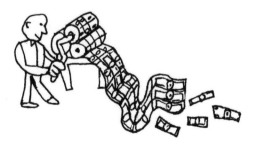

In many ways, Twain is the patron saint of the not rich, routinely investing his money in things that would never bring him wealth. He even invested his wife's inheritance in inventions that he was certain would change the world but didn't, not even a little. At one point, after investing in the Kaolatype, which was invented by a friend of Twain's who had already run one business into the ground, Twain asked to see a demonstration of this engraving machine he had invested in. The night before Twain was to visit, the shop burned down. Twain made a second appointment, this time to visit the inventor's own shop, and, again, the night before he was to visit, the place burned down. And yet Twain's optimism toward the investment continued. Even after he realized that his old friend had probably been keeping two sets of books, that the patent for the Kaolatype was a fraud, Twain still believed in the Kaolatype machine itself—an illustration of how to never, ever get rich. Later, Twain would fail at other endeavors, including as a publisher, despite publishing his own books. "I must speculate in something, such being my nature," Twain wrote.[7] At Twain's funeral, which was coincidentally on Shakespeare's birthday, William Dean Howells, as if speaking of the successful nonrich everywhere, said, "We may confess that he had faults, while we deny that he tried to pass them as merits. He disowned his errors by owning them; in the very defects of his qualities he triumphed, and he could make us glad with him at his escape from them."

Being a writer in itself may have helped Twain achieve these pinnacles of nonrich greatness. That writers are not prone to wealth creation was also proved by James Joyce, who, while well known for *Ulysses*, the famed stream-of-consciousness novel that made him a little bit of snot-green cash after years of having none at all, is rightfully not remembered for opening Dublin's first movie theater, which showed only films in Italian and, naturally, closed immediately. But is there a point to be made here about being a great writer and not making money? As a professional writer, I would say I don't think so. I would say that some guys know how to not make money, and some guys don't. Those other guys just have to find a way to come to terms with that.

LOOKING AT ONE'S OWN PERSONAL NONRICH HISTORY can be especially illuminating to the person seeking not to accumulate wealth on an unprecedented scale. Yes, it is true that the possibility of "getting rich" is dangled before us as we make our way through a life lined with insurance premiums, but the attainment of such a state is kept at a distance that, while it can sometimes seem to be decreasing, never actually decreases, along the lines of Zeno's paradox. Often, in closely examining our own personal unwealthy history, one sees that the road that is one's past is chock-full of places we only now realize were exits to the (really) good life. In other words, we realize, in retrospect, that we blew it.

This idea—that we blew it—is based on the not-rich person's theory of history, which says that history is like one of those space-time continuums that you might see in a science fiction movie or in a young person's outrageously expensive video game, only it's a money-time continuum. In the money-time continuum, there are invisible portals, and the portals open to a path in life that leads to the big buckaroos, to early retirement, to worry-free existence. If you are smart, you don't miss a portal, especially since there aren't that many portals. The very rich can sense the presence of a portal, or so the not very rich believe. The not very rich, on the other hand, might not know a portal if

it came to their door dressed as Ed McMahon and carrying a giant million-dollar check with the not-rich person's name on it.

The money-time continuum theory is generally espoused late in the evening or at bars and typically begins with a phrases such as "If I'd only . . ." Examples include "If only I'd realized he was offering me stock . . ." or "If only I'd been able to get the money together for a down payment on that waterfront property . . ." or "If only I'd taken that job with my friend's then-unknown uncle, Warren Buffet . . ." It is not uncommon for the not rich to believe that the rich get better at seeing the portals the more they enter them. Conversely, the nonrich often feel that once you miss a portal, it becomes more and more difficult to identify the next one.

A case study is that of one forty-one-year-old male, a married father of two. Each month, while paying a rent that he would not wish on a cruel Roman emperor, he is often reminded of the very first apartment he'd lived in with his wife. It was in a good neighborhood. It was big. His wife's former roommate was about to abandon the building. They could have taken the apartment over; most likely, they could even have bought their apartment. They could then have lived there with kids, so roomy was the apartment, such a nice neighborhood was it set in, so perfect. The husband, however, felt that there would be more and better opportunities for places to live, though that would not turn out to be the case. They considered staying and renting, but he "didn't feel like it," or something like that. The exact words are not available to sociologists or to me—as a result, the forty-one-year-old male is sometimes forced to imagine possible alternative versions over and over. To be sure, he knows that whatever he said, it was not the right thing. To his enduring frustration, he does remember that his wife suggested they stay. It is clear to the forty-one-year-old husband only now that his wife recognized a time-money continuum, an on-ramp to financial security. And this is not the only thing that she has recognized and he has missed, believe me.

I have taken up the issue of history as it relates to how not to get rich, and at this point I had intended to arrive at a conclusion of some significance regarding history and the nonaccumulation of financial wealth. I see now, though, that I have arrived at a point about listening to the person that you are married to.

How to Cultivate the Attitude That Will Lead to Not Getting Rich

BEFORE WE examine the more practical maneuvers that can keep you from becoming really, really wealthy, let us first consider the almost ineffable—let us consider the mind-set of the successful nonbillionaire. To be successful at not being famously or even mildly famously rich, one must cultivate the nonrich mind-set with persistence and

in a relaxed, easygoing manner. What is the nonrich mind-set? Often it is the mind-set equated with the disgruntled worker, the shrill and pessimistic loner who believes he or she has been, in the parlance of the stereotypical disgruntled American, "screwed over." The "screwed over" nonrich mind-set operates on the belief that he or she has been "screwed over" by one of any number of entities he or she deems more powerful than him- or herself—a long list of organizations and individuals that includes but is not limited to any combination of the following: the government, corporations, the System, life, the United Nations, his or her former best friend, the guy he or she sat next to at a baseball game who has a chain of car dealerships and didn't return his or her call, God, some jerk, mothers-in-law, and the IRS. This is the nonrich mind-set most frequently portrayed on television and in films, usually with guns and explosive devices strapped to the disgruntled person in question. The more prevalent nonrich mind-set, however, is one of subdued resignation, a trait that makes for a quiet undercurrent in the sea of American life. If I could afford a poll, I'll bet I could show that this latter nonrich mind-set is the nonrich mind-set of the vast majority of Americans.[8]

In fact, this particular nonrich mind-set is like second nature to most people, requiring little work or focused practice besides some shrugging now and then, but it is by no means automatic—it should not be neglected or counted on, for it is precisely by *not* cultivating this mind-set that many of the most recently self-made millionaires have failed. The reason that a person might neglect to practice a nonrich mind-set is that it is a relatively new phenomenon in American life. Recall that after World War II, Americans worked hard and ended up with cars and mortgages and were able to retire without being J. P. Morgan. And it was

not as if Americans all had secondary degrees in finance
with which to pursue a higher standard of living; they came
out of the war and worked in factories or in midlevel office
jobs and drank a lot, even at lunch. Yes, our forefathers and
foremothers were, in a sense, able to live much better than
we are now—from a wage-earning and job-security per-
spective, at least—even while drunk. Meanwhile, we tee-
total our way into insolvency, attempting, though often
failing, to watch our weight as well. Forty years ago, people
were served well with an everybody-will-be-pretty-well-off
mind-set. Today, people are not served nearly as well with
an everybody-is-getting-less mind-set, but this mind-set
will nevertheless help prevent *you* from getting rich—the
end result for the average American, if we play our cards
right, being that we will live longer with fewer health
benefits.

In other words, when calibrating your own personal
financial mind-set, it is today more appropriate to expect
the *reverse* of what your parents expected and act accord-
ingly—and there are several ways to do this so that you
don't get rich. The simplest way is by merely comparing
your situation with the situation of most other people in
the world, a kind of preventive empathy that is a variation
on a move from the parenting playbook of yesteryear—
e.g., "Eat your brussels sprouts because there are children
in India who don't have brussels sprouts!" In adult life, this
strategy works like this: The person who is never going to
be a majority stockholder in a large corporation picks up a
newspaper, reads about disease and rising unemployment
and personal freedoms being eroded around the globe, or
the disparity between people who have access to resources
and capital and those who don't. This person then merely
compares his own situation with the situation of this vast
number of others. This may sound complicated, or perhaps

inane, but the result is that, even though you are not a millionaire and have no health insurance, no retirement fund, and your landlord is knocking on the front door, you suddenly see your own situation in a more positive light, thus eliminating the desire to make a killing on the stock market or to make a killing on anything really, at least for that day. In operating thusly, you admire and savor your $4 gourmet coffee drink, while getting a little closer to understanding the piece of your personal portfolio that the philosopher Thomas Merton called "this little point of nothingness and of absolute poverty."

Remember: People who risk getting rich may pick up the paper and immediately see opportunity for wealth making. Of course, some individuals can simultaneously read the paper and sense that their own situations are not that bad in comparison to others *and* make a killing. Take George Soros, to pick one socially conscious multibillionaire financial investor. Soros invests his money in solving the above-mentioned world problems *and* makes a killing on the markets.[9] Indeed, in thinking of Soros, one is reminded of Thoreau, who, in "Civil Disobedience," wrote, "The best thing a man can do for his culture when he is rich is to endeavor to carry out those schemes which he

entertained when he was poor."* At least I am reminded of Thoreau when I think of Soros. I am also reminded, as a successful nonrich person myself, of how much I am not like George Soros.

But I digress—and in so doing have inadvertently raised another crucial point. For when considering exactly how George Soros reads the paper, I can only guess that he skips the comics, but in merely guessing that a socially conscious billionaire skips the comics, in pondering this very topic at length, or pondering other topics like it at similarly lengthy intervals, I am cultivating an excellent

---

* In contrast, probably one of the worst things that a man can do when he is not rich is to endeavor to carry out those schemes of somebody whose income is three or four times greater. How often do we who are successfully not rich act as if we were unsuccessful at being not rich? How many people who just order two appetizers when out to dinner go home to a $12,000 designer refrigerator—a refrigerator that you could put on a nice piece of land and even live in if it had just a little better ventilation—to keep the doggie bag in? An example I am thinking of that relates here involves an artist whom I'll call Scott because that's his name. He bought tiles for his kitchen counter that cost him— well, I don't have the exact figures in front of me, but it wasn't quite what the Explorer program cost NASA. Anyway, he bought these incredibly expensive tiles for his kitchen counter—and I'm not saying he doesn't deserve these tiles, because I actually think we all deserve incredibly expensive handmade tiles—and now he finds that not only can he not cut vegetables or execute anything cooking-related on them, but the cost of maintaining them makes it a good thing he can't cut vegetables on them because when he's all done taking care of the tiles and not cutting up anything on them, he simply has no more money left for food. On the other hand, the tiles look terrific.

non-Big-Money-making mind-set. Indeed, if I spent just a few minutes every day attempting to figure out whether a billionaire would read the comics just on Sunday or during the week or maybe online, if he reads the comics at all, I end up with (1) a somewhat incomplete and thus unful-filling conclusion, and (2) no actual increase in my per-sonal wealth. In fact, I probably even lost money, given that I am self-employed.

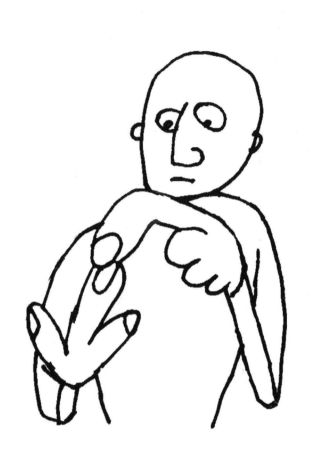

How to Act in Given Situations While Attempting to Cultivate the Attitude That Will Lead to Not Getting Rich

IN STAYING off the Fortune 500 list, it is important to carry yourself like someone who is not going to get extremely rich very, very quickly, or possibly at any time. The body and all its actions must express what the mind believes, which is that there is no way in hell you are ever going to live in a mansion, and that even if you did, you wouldn't know what to do with yourself and would end up walking from room to room just looking around, nervous. Befuddlement is a good default emotional setting. When shopping, for instance, take as much time as possible in making choices that really don't matter but are unavoidable because we live in a consumerist society that is based on offering people more products than they can even handle.[10] And most importantly, don't consider the world yours for the taking. Try thinking of the world as the opposite once in a while—i.e., yours for the leaving the way you found it when you got here or, more simply, not just yours.

How does the person who is not going to get rich act in particular everyday circumstances wherein he or she might in some way reap great financial reward or any reward, really? To answer this question, consider the following hypothetical situation and decide on the appropriate never-going-to-get-rich response. The hypothetical situation: a fender bender. The scene: the parking lot at the Shop N' Save. The action begins as a senior driver, venturing to the supermarket after her Meals-On-Wheels program is cut, attempts to pull out of her parking spot into the parking lot filled with people who, despite being in a parking lot, seem to be driving as fast as they can. Suddenly, a box of unsalted saltines tumbles from a bag

on the senior driver's front seat, causing her concentration to break and, as a result, her foot to hit the gas and then the brake, the gas-then-brake process repeated in a confused and herky-jerky fashion until the driver accidentally slams into the back of your 1989 Toyota Camry, the rear bumper of which is still suffering from the time you ran it into your neighbor's SUV, a car named for a Western state because it's the same size as one. And now the question—as far as general comportment goes, which conduct is more appropriate for the never, ever rich?

(a) While immediately commencing to seethe with anger, since this incident will cause you to be late for your eleven A.M. meeting, you slam your hand on the horn so forcefully that the air bag inflates. At which point you wrestle yourself from the car and, at the top of your lungs, suggest (even as you

inspect the "damage," which is more cosmetic than structural, more scratch among scratches) that the senior citizen—who is trembling now and worried and being tsk-tsked by the blood-smelling mob assembling in the Shop N' Save lot—will soon be hearing from your attorney, who, as you shall instruct him, will not only be suing her but will win the suit at nearly any cost, and, you hope, reap rewards that, while not unheard of in the annals of legal history, will move you toward your ultimate goal, which is general wealth improvement. The woman gets back in her car and sits there staring ahead as you raise your hand in victory upon returning to your air-bag-deflated car. You then recite aloud the words of Sophocles Publius Sirius, the Roman scholar who no doubt had to deal with this kind of thing (seniors) while being a scholar in ancient Rome: "Fortune is not on the side of the fainthearted."

(b) You roll your eyes, take a deep breath, feel the warm wash of something gone wrong wash over you and (as often happens if you give it a chance) pass away. At which point you look into the rearview mirror to see the senior citizen with her head in her hands, the salt-free saltines forgotten, the fear building—a sight that, in turn, causes you to think of how your own mother or grandmother might react, how she might be panic-stricken if she had hit a car (assuming she would have noticed)—so that you slowly step from your car and, with the widest smile you can muster, with exaggerations of extremely positive body language, assist the woman from her car and inspect the damage, which might seem signifi-cant to a passerby who did not know that your car

had 258,000 miles on it, but is really nothing to you.
And then, like more Americans than the press or the
current administration would have you believe, you
do *not* sue, a word so rich, so full of promise, to the
wannabe wealthy, and simultaneously so meaningless to the wannabe not rich.[11]

The correct answer is *b*, of course, and while this may be an
intellectually simple choice, it is not as simple a choice in a
real-life situation. Role-playing can help. Get together
with friends who have never owned a vacation place in
the Caribbean and try acting out everyday scenes in which
you might be tempted to act with a wealth-inducing
attitude but ultimately do not. I am compelled to say that
there is a market for personal trainers specializing in
helping you carry yourself as if you are not going to
get rich, but that might mean that some motivated person
reading this would actually pursue such an opportunity
and subsequently franchise the idea and then, next thing

you know, another person is loaded, possibly even me. No, I will avoid *that* temptation.

Ultimately, at the center of any nonrich routine is the unwavering belief (or hardly-ever-wavering belief) that somehow, in some way—just as their nonmillionaire parents told them, just as people feel once in a while when the coffee wears off and the world seems momentarily calm and peaceful, just as they have to believe late at night if they are ever going to get some sleep or even any sleep at all—everything will be all right.

How to Choose a Career That Will Not Get You Rich No Matter What Anyone Tells You

Choosing a career path is essential to implementing a spot that is not in the top 2 percent of American incomes or anywhere near it, and an essential part of choosing the right career is choosing the right kind of education. These days, a good education is a must if you are planning on working your entire life and ending up with little or nothing. History tells us that at one time only the wealthiest Americans had a college education, and the people who did not go to college made money working in factory jobs that today no longer exist. Now you need a college education to work on the line in one of the few remaining auto plants, if you can afford a college education, that is. If you do manage to wrangle the absurdly large loans necessary to fund a trip to college, then, to not succeed financially, you will want to choose a field of study that will be personally rewarding but have no apparent application in the real world. Here are just a few possibilities:

Medieval literature. This is a wonderful area of essentially not-for-profit study, and, indeed, a study of just medieval poetry will only reinforce the improbability of retiring on what you will earn, even though you may see the world as a more beautiful place, and, through the sight of such beauty, you will be stock-poor but soul-enhanced. In addition to translating wonderful but sensationally obscure poems that could never be valued in accordance with their aesthetic worth, other areas of unprofitable expertise would include the study of medieval literary figures themselves, such as Alcuin, the once world-renowned and now not-so-well-known tutor to Charlemagne, who, excitingly, had a school of scholars translating and copying ancient texts in medieval France, and who reignited interest in Greek and Roman classics in Europe, giving us a glimpse back into a time when the world was smaller and you could retire to your kids' villa, rather than be forced to begin to apply to assisted-living places when you are in your forties in hopes of getting a spot that you probably won't be able to afford one day. Alcuin, who also tutored Pippin, the son of Charlemagne, rediscovered Socratic dialogue as a teaching method, so that the following questions might be offered to the following responses in the eighth century A.D.:

PIPPIN: What is a letter?
ALCUIN: The guardian of history.
PIPPIN: What is a word?
ALCUIN: The expositor of the mind.

PIPPIN: What produces a word?

ALCUIN: The tongue.

PIPPIN: What is the tongue?

ALCUIN: The whip of the air.

PIPPIN: What is the air?

ALCUIN: The guardian of life.

PIPPIN: What is life?

ALCUIN: The joy of the blessed, the sorrow of the miserable, the expectation of death.

PIPPIN: What is death?

ALCUIN: The inevitable issue, an uncertain pilgrimage, the tears of the living, the thief of man.

PIPPIN: What is man?

ALCUIN: The possession of death, a transient wayfarer, a guest.

PIPPIN: How is man situated?

ALCUIN: Like a lantern in the wind.

Magnificent, and it notably does not end the way a financial investment company's commercials typically end. You know the financial investment company commercials I'm referring to. They feature a long, sentimental, and joyful montage of images that portray the imaginary life you would have if you had nothing to worry about money-wise: sailing, croquet on the lawn of the beach house, sentimental gazes between well-dressed family members. Then, the ad ends with the logo of the financial investment company, the message being something along the lines of this: *Don't you want to have a really amazing life, as far as material goods go, or do you have some kind of a problem?*

If you should actually go into medieval studies, then your only real worry is that a huge movie star—say he has his car parked by the guy you sat next to in the waiting room of the downtown health clinic—hears about your obscure area of expertise, becomes enamored with Alcuin while on location in France, gets a kind of over-glamorized view of what it was like to run a medieval school of classical scholarship during the Holy Roman Empire, shows up with his entourage at your library cubicle one afternoon, lunches you, hires you as a consultant, makes a film in which the scene that you worked hardest on (where rows of robed scholars sat quietly copying ancient texts) is cut, after which you appear on a public television talk show to praise the movie's accuracy, after which you are offered your own television show on cable, which subsequently spawns best-selling books and CD-ROMs and a Wednesday spot on the *Today* show that features you translating French medieval lyrics for the viewers at home. Granted, that scenario is not incredibly likely, but it's a possibility, and to live the not-rich life completely, you have to stay on your toes.

Wildlife biologist. As far as not making it big goes, studies of flora and fauna are especially unlucrative, despite that flora and fauna are seemingly the most related to the world, or at least the living, breathing world. Why? Because they investigate an area that the economic system considers unprofitable—i.e., natural life. If you played your cards "right," you could spend years in graduate school studying biology and then finally manage to cobble together grant money to pursue your area of interest—Pacific-coast sea otters (*Enhydra lutris*), let's say, hunted into near extinction in the eighteen hundreds for their pelts despite being, as can unprofitably be noted, one of the few mammals besides

humans to use tools.[12] You will live in a tent in the cold
watching a small radar screen indicating the location of the
sea otter that you have forcibly but lovingly tagged, and you
will make important discoveries about the animal's migra-
tory patterns, and then your studies will be discounted by
cruise ship and real estate interests. (Caution: Oil companies
sometimes hire wildlife biologists, decorating oil-interested
company reports with otter-friendly statistics that are subsequently ignored when drilling time comes.)

Traditional music. This is an excellent area of unprofitable
possibilities, especially in light of today's popular music,
which can, in many instances, be explained as multimil-
lion-dollar marketing set to a computer-generated sound
track—which is to say the sound track of a corporation
raking it in. In some ways, someone choosing to become a
professional hammer dulcimer player is the opposite of
someone choosing a career that statistics indicate will
manage to keep him or her alive—careers such as health
care, education, and engineering, all of which are recom-
mended by career planners and require advanced degrees
that you will be paying for over many, many years.[13] Have
you ever seen a mandolin player with a yacht? Do you
know many full-time jug-band members with 401(k)

plans? Is there in America today a professional penny-whistle player who has two homes and a condo on Central Park West in Manhattan? Do people who make their living as accordionists fly first-class out of LAX? No, in fact people with accordions are the butt of jokes even from other traditional musicians, implying a lowest-man-on-the-lowest-totem-pole status that can be applauded in the area of not getting fantastically rich. Some gratuitous accordion joke examples are as follows:

> Q: What's the difference between an onion and an accordion?
> A: People cry when they chop up onions.
> Q: What do you call ten accordions at the bottom of the ocean?
> A: A good start.
> Q: If you drop an accordion, a set of bagpipes, and a viola off a twenty-story building, which one lands first?
> A: Who cares?[14]

THERE ARE, OF COURSE, AN INFINITE NUMBER of non-wealth-producing careers to choose from. There's public broadcasting, wherein the person involved attempts to create radio and television programs that will attract viewers interested in a broad range of subjects that may not titillate advertisers, the core audience, it sometimes seems, for non-public broadcasting. There are more obvious examples, such as teaching, which has to do with the joy of learning and with the education of the next generation of adults, as well as the future of the economy and of the world. There is art that has no wide commercial appeal. There is commerce that has no wide commercial appeal but works on a limited basis in a limited area for a limited number of people until a chain store hears about it and comes in and takes over, putting everyone else out of business. In other words, the options for non-Big-Buck-making careers are wide-ranging. The one universally important thing to keep in mind when choosing a career that will not be making you loaded is to choose a field of study and expertise that interests you, to follow your passions—and unless your passion is making lots of money, you will be fairly assured of not getting rich. Ralph Waldo Emerson said, "The reward of doing a thing well is to have done it," and he had a point, though he is not factoring in the cost of child care, studio space, and gas, or even parking, all of which really add up.

How to Choose an Investment Strategy That Will Definitely Not Get You Rich

THERE ARE two basic investment strategies that will definitely not get you rich. The first is to follow the herd. This is done by hiring a broker who couldn't get a job out of college (but was smart enough not to become a writer) and so became a broker. He invests your meager savings in an investment that thousands and thousands of other people are investing in. Next, due to the lemminglike run on this particular investment by all the brokers and their clients, you all lose your shirts.

The second strategy is to have absolutely no investment strategy. Government bonds, 401(k)'s, hedge funds, time-released securities, security-released times—commonly, they are all as nothing to those who are not on the road

to huge financial gain.[15] This second
strategy is the one most frequently
used by the most successful unrich,
but it is not as simple as it sounds,
given that the noninvestor is
surrounded by the siren call of
the investment, not to mention the call
of all those bogus Internet investment
scams that people actually buy into. Day
to day, those avoiding investment entirely generally don't
get rich by living paycheck to paycheck. In fact, within this
nonstrategy strategy are several substrategies designed
either to take your mind off the fact that you do not have
an investment strategy or to just give
your mind some time off. They
include:

(a) Hang out in the park playing
    Frisbee golf all weekend long and
    then panic on Sunday night as
    you finally go through the bills the
    day before they are due.
(b) Spend a lot of money express-mailing
    checks that are late.

(c) Try to figure out how you are going to pay the rent or the mortgage or the bill for the credit card due any minute and realize you used the money you could have used to make the car payment *last* month. Then come up with enough cash at the very last 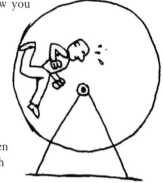 minute, at which point you begin the process again. (Typically, those who are most successful in not cleaning up spend their money paying more to spend the money they don't have—a structural bummer, as far as the inherent quality of the economy goes.)[16]

(d) Don't let your lack of investment strategy bother you too much, since you are working hard, working two jobs maybe, working on the weekends in some cases, and, when you have time off, you don't want to think about money, you just want to relax a little, with not-for-profit oil painting or Scrabble.

(e) Give up even trying to understand how you are ever going to come up with a successful life financial plan, as happened recently at a dinner party in a suburban town where a man that I will call Fred sat across from an investment banker who has asked to be identified only as Don and who went on at length about a particular type of bond and used the term *aggressive strategy*, which means a lot to many, many people, but pretty much nothing to Fred, who, at some point kind of checked out and

began wondering which was better, *Led Zeppelin II*
or *Led Zeppelin III.*

A variation on the noninvestment investment strategy is
the overexamination strategy. Utilizing this strategy, a
person is extremely careful with his or her money, making
painstakingly cautious decisions, watching it closely, meticulously, only to realize at some point that it is gone.
Though psychologically complicated, this is a nearly
surefire way to not get rich. Thomas Jefferson is a case
in point here. This founding father was a manic accountant,
a trait he'd picked up from *his* father. He accounted for
everything all through his life, right down to the paper,
quill, and ink he used to account for everything. (Jefferson
devised our national accounting strategy, proposing the
decimal accounting of dollars and cents.) He considered
himself personally thrifty, and he vigorously protested and
during his term literally reduced government debt, even
though the Louisiana Purchase was something the United
States probably shouldn't have purchased, or at least
couldn't afford, a national impulse buy. Meanwhile, Jefferson had a nonthrifty streak, a passion that contradicted
his tendency to account for everything—a crucial element
in this bad-investment strategy. Jefferson was an enthu-
siastic naturalist. Once, while ambassador to France, he
met the famous French naturalist Georges de Buffon,
who, Jefferson felt, was misinformed about many American
species, including the moose. Buffon thought the moose on
the smallish side, like a deer. Jefferson knew the moose to be
big, like a moose. They disputed the size of moose horns.
Jefferson wrote to John Sullivan, a general during the
Revolutionary War who was by then governor of New
Hampshire, and asked him to bag a moose. Sullivan sent out
a party of hunters to Maine. They bagged a moose and sent

its skin, skeleton, and horns to Jefferson in France. The bill arrived first: forty-five pounds, a huge sum. Even now, I can hear Jefferson taking a big gulp as he peruses the bill. Then the moose arrived. Its horns were disappointingly small. Jefferson had to apologize to Buffon, forty-five pounds down the drain.

At the end of his life, Jefferson was still obsessively accounting for everything, logging numbers in his so-called *Farm Book.* "[A] gallon of lamp oil, costing $1.25, has lighted my chamber highly 25 nights, for six hours a night, which is 5 cents [a night] for 150 hours . . . ," read his last entry in his *Farm Book.* Near his death, the *Farm Book* showed him to be $107,000 in debt and surrounded by land-rich, cash-poor farmers about to go under, after the Panic of 1819. Jefferson pushed for the Virginia legislature to allow him to run a lottery to sell off part of his land to clear his debts, even though he had himself long opposed lotteries and banned the use of playing cards and dice at the University of Virginia. Many Virginia legislators were against the idea, so to convince them Jefferson cataloged his years of public service, public service itself being a recipe for financial ruin when served virtuously. "Public service and private misery are inseparably linked together," Jefferson wrote.[17] In the end, the legislature allowed Jefferson his land lottery.

Speaking of land, we must consider real estate as a dubious investment strategy for those seeking to be *un*-loaded. Late-night TV seminars teach us that real estate means wealth. Yes, you could buy trumped-up vacation land that turns out to be a decades-old toxic-waste dumping site, though this was not made clear to you at the time you bought it at an incredibly cheap price on the Internet, and then you could, as a result, become bankrupt. Yes, you could even buy at the top of a bubble that is about to burst, whatever that means. But more likely the value of land you bought will continue to increase, especially as land every-where on the planet is furiously bought up by varied corporate interests.

Unfortunately, you can't just not invest to not get rich; you have to spend unwisely. A great way to do this is to make occasional shopping sprees on behalf of family members or loved ones—purchases of gifts that you can't afford but that will touch that person forever, the way you will be touched forever by the payments on your credit card.

What I'm saying is that you have to think big about thinking small. In the end, you want to create a lifestyle that is not oriented toward huge profits at all. If you own your own business, you want to resist the urge to invest in your own workplace and transform it from a small place

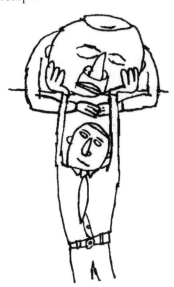

that makes enough to get by and to keep the workforce happy and stocked up with benefits into a giant factory that makes a lot of money and gets bought out so that you alone are then able to move to Palm Springs.[18] As a consumer, you want to avoid buying cheaply in bulk at stores that are as big as aircraft hangars, as well as spend your money in a manner that would be unreasonable to any money manager worth his commission. As a non-millionaire-to-be consumer, you want to shop at a smaller store, a boutique or shop even, a place where you might know the proprietor and other customers, a place where you will pay the proprietor more in the way of prices so that he can continue in a line of work that, given the pressure of the nearby megastore, will certainly get him not rich in a real hurry. Done right, not getting rich can be a neighborhood process, a group thing, in which everyone doesn't get rich together.

A Brief Note on the Importance of Upbringing; or, Are We Born Unrich?

It almost goes without saying that it helps to have a healthy non-Big-Money-oriented upbringing. It helps, for example, when you are raised by people who worked hard and managed to stay alive but did not rake it in as some people around them did. It helps to have been raised by people who saw money as a thing that could taint people, which it does not. As it turns out, it sometimes seems as if not having money probably taints more than the other way around, and the therapy and personal reflection that this emotional issue in itself requires sure helps keep the dough not rolling in.

As an economic society, we are like a family that doesn't know whether we want to be rich like the neighbors or whether we want to just sit around alternately lauding and criticizing those who are doing pretty nicely. As a society,

we are sometimes like the older sibling who says to the younger, "Wow, you bought a fancy car! I could have bought a fancy car but I chose to spend the money I could have spent on a fancy car on charitable causes instead. But, hey, your car looks great!" As a society, we are like the younger sibling who at a party says, "Oh, yeah my sister's great!"—and then in the privacy of her morning espresso drink line declares to her office mate that her sister is *nuts* to spend all that money on the trip to the Bahamas when their parents are living with a broken dishwasher. We are also like the brother who never writes. We as an economic society are further like a family in that we have borrowed money from each other and have now forgotten to pay it back; and in that we think we know what's going on money-wise with the person or people living down the street or in another state, when in fact we don't. We, the people whose income levels continue to drop in real terms, are lastly like a family in that we can be good together but also need some time apart—we can make it if we step back and let some things go and realize that society is what *we* make of it. Because the truth is, unlike an actual family, society mostly doesn't really care about you at all. In society's default mode, when you *don't* make anything of society, society couldn't care less. Of course, this will make things easier for you if you are not trying to get rich. Society won't be getting in your way.

Still, this is the United States of America, and non-millionaires are made here as well as just born. We need only look at such things as offtrack betting and the success of state departments of education that finance the education of our young people through the taxation of huge twenty-four-hour casinos to know that government not only counts on but in some ways *depends* on some people to spend their entire lives attempting to get rich and, in so doing, inadvertently succeed handsomely in not getting rich. Truly many of our governments, state, local, and even federal, are working with us (in some weird way) to become not rich. Surely, there is hope for all Americans. Yes, the road to not getting rich is full of roadblocks and pitfalls, but have faith ye who are not yet not well-off, for you can stumble ass backward over the finish line.

Another Brief Note, This Time on Loyalty, Which Seems to Pertain to Our Goal, Though Perhaps Only Tangentially

IT MUST be stated flatly that one should not trust loyalty alone to keep you from being situated financially such that you are able to buy a Greek island. Loyalty is one of those things that on paper doesn't add up to much, and, though you can spend a good deal of time searching through the pages of history for someone who made a lot of money being loyal, you are more likely to find a lot written on people who broke off, who said to hell with it and left the team and went on to make a lot of money at another place and never saw their old friends again. *Et tu, Brute* is a phrase that springs to mind, though disloyalty is not usually so much about the *dis*. It's about change, about seizing a seemingly better opportunity, and this kind of not-so-loyal behavior happens all the time, leading to wealth *and* not to wealth, depending. It can be argued that in most businesses today, advancement is absolutely *dependent* on disloyalty, on you leaving the team behind. Disloyalty is expected, and if you don't consider it an option, even your closest friends and workmates will begin to look at you and wonder if your organic yogurt has begun to react negatively with your cortex.

But if you stick with your buddies through *their* non-moneymaking processes, if you stay with the team when the team is down, or even if you start transferring funds from your savings account to the account that you use to shower your great-grandmother with things she doesn't need but loves (a version of familial loyalty, I suppose), then you will find that loyalty is one of those qualities that when put together with other things—obliviousness, trust, inability to read the stock pages—can aid significantly in your pursuit of unbillions.

Take Ulysses S. Grant, a great general and a really lousy businessman, in large part because he was too loyal. Before the Civil War he tried farming and proved he was a bad farmer. Then he moved to St. Louis, where he got a job in real estate and proved he was a bad real-estate salesman. Except for the part where he hoped he could make a living, his heart wasn't in real estate or any business at all. The story is told of one particular real estate transaction in St. Louis, a building sale that Grant was brokering and, thus, fell through. One day, the guy Grant was selling the building to approached Grant on the street to tell him that he was considering purchasing another building. Upon hearing the news, Grant, rather than negotiate, turned and walked away; according to a bystander, Grant looked as if he were about to cry. Then came the Civil War, which he won, partly because of his loyal commanders, and then came his administration, which was marked by the scandals of people he perhaps *over*trusted. Then came his life after office, at which point he was looking to finally make a good living. Grant met a guy on Wall Street, Ferdinand Ward, a guy he trusted, a guy known in the late 1870s as "the Napoleon of Wall Street," a guy who subsequently used Grant's name to great harm-causing effect. Grant had his wife invest all her money in the firm of Grant & Ward. He had his sisters invest their money in Grant & Ward. Grant's son, who had introduced his father to Ferdinand Ward, did the same. Soon enough, Grant & Ward went bust. Grant couldn't believe it and, for a short time, didn't believe it— he had planned on finally striking it big when in fact he lost everything. (Some sources wonder whether Grant knew what was going on, whether the general was in on a scam,

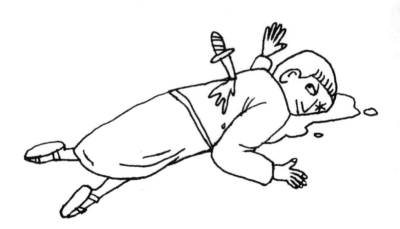

but Grant sounds to me like a bit of a sucker, which I mean in the best possible way.)

The rest of Grant's story works against the idea of loyalty as a pure path to poverty. After Grant & Ward crashed, Cornelius Vanderbilt, the then mogul, lent Grant money, and Grant, ever honorable, insisted on giving Vanderbilt his home, his farm, and all his personal belongings, including swords and medals of honor and commendations. Things did not look good for Grant, at which point he contracted throat cancer. To get his family out of debt, Grant wrote a memoir, something he hadn't wanted to do, which once again stinks of loyalty to me. Grant dictated the memoir until he became so ill that he had to handwrite the rest. "The writing of the *Memoirs* was a race with death," one biographer wrote. "He hoped that the book would provide something for his wife to live on after he had gone, and he clung desperately to this earth until the manuscript was completed." Grant died when he was done, carrying a note to his wife in his pocket—a wish to meet again in a better world. His memoir was a best seller.

That the memoir was a best seller is additionally

amazing, in terms of the annals of not getting rich, in that the memoirs were published by Mark Twain, who, as we have already noted, had the opposite of a golden touch. In assisting Grant, Twain came to respect the old general, to admire him for what Twain called "honor, duty, country"—the very aspects of loyalty to community that Twain had questioned as a young writer. Twain put all of his own money into the project, and he published Grant's memoirs immediately after Grant died on July 23, 1885. Twain paid Grant's widow $400,000 and was himself for the first time debt-free.

DESPITE THE OCCASIONAL BOOM IN material wealth that comes from loyalty, loyalty is mostly discounted in books full of quotes that are supposed to inspire us to a wealth-inducing lifestyle. Niccolò Machiavelli made a career out of preaching that kind of thing (or preaching against it, if you see *The Prince* as a satire on a corrupt political system, as I do). "Teamwork?" goes a quote often attributed to Somerset Maugham. "Whoever heard of making a fortune by teamwork? There's only one way to make a fortune, and that's to down the fellow who's up against you." And yet when I investigate Maugham's attitude, I learn that he broke down in tears while on the radio reading a passage from the very book that this quote is taken from, a passage he had based on the life of his mother. Then again, that's a problem with aphorisms. You can't really sum up the grayness of life, its entropically uncoordinatable nature. About aphorisms generally, I know that Groucho Marx was once quoted as saying the following: "Quote me as saying, 'I was misquoted.'"*

* I feel as though—to be a self-respecting self-help-book author—I ought to have at least one quote from Scripture, so here goes mine, which is from the Song of Songs: "Feast, friends, and drink till you are drunk with love."

How to Spend the Bulk of Your Leisure Time If You Are Not Going to Get Rich, Probably Ever

You READ. You read for pleasure. Not constantly; you want to see your friends and get outside once in a while and so on, but you want to do a lot of reading. Perhaps it sounds too simple, but reading is an important strategy in the pursuit of a lifestyle that is, monetarily speaking, not that well-off. Reading is problematic as a nonwealth generator, however, and it should be stressed that reading is strewn with potential moneymaking fodder—i.e., business books, a broad category that I use to define books that seek to improve your financial situation, whether as an investor, a corporate worker, or a CEO. It is no surprise that business books are among the best-selling books in America today, and, yes, if you read a business book that purports to engender positive life-changing or moneymaking attitudes or one that offers successful strategies for pulling down the wonder bucks, and, yes, if you then proceed to actually adopt those attitudes and strategies, then, yes, you might actually make some money. To avoid this scenario and continue to not get rich you have several options:

(a) Buy the book that aims to help you revamp your moneymaking lifestyle and then do not read it, adding it instead to the long list of things that you have not done—a list that everyone who is no-where near a millionaire continually cultivates.

(b) Buy the book and read it, then buy another book and read it, and continue buying books—books such as *Execution: The Discipline of Getting Things Done* and *Purple Cow: Transform Your Business by Being Remarkable* (actual titles). Repeat the process so that you end up becoming a How-to-Get Rich hobbyist, an expert on ways to achieve immeasurable fortune, a person who is so completely keyed into the moneymaking trends that he or she, rather than making money, spends his or her time critiquing moneymaking options and painting a never-finished picture for him- or herself of the *ideal* moneymaking job or career path, which either does not exist or has evaporated in the time that this person has spent analyzing the ways in which he or she might finally really make some real money, as in millions.

(c) Merely muse on business book titles, a favorite pastime of this author. Additional actual, un-made-up examples include *Who Moved the Cheese?* and *Fish!* and

Mentored by a Millionaire.[19] These titles are enter-
taining in themselves and say something about the
nature of business books, whatever that is.

But just reading—reading for pleasure, reading a novel
while you are on the bus or the train or the subway,
reading a biography instead of returning *all* your boss's e-
mails, reading philosophy in the back of a seminar that
your corporate team sent you to, reading in the coffee shop
a short prose poem translated from Spanish by your
favorite Chilean playwright, reading a movie review while
standing online at the place where you pay bills when you
are too late to mail them—just reading novels and books in
general will greatly aid you in your pursuit to not be rich,
if only in their sheer time-as-money-wasting capacity. It
makes a practicing nonbazillionaire such as myself tremble
to consider how much money I could lose reading *Anna
Karenina!*

And don't forget poetry, that seemingly forgotten
form that makes so little money for big publishing
corporations but amazingly will not die. Poetry is something no self-respecting billionaire-to-be would tie his
financial ambitions to, even if there is little fear of a
repossession of a villanelle. Poetry is itself a metaphor-
ical model for how not to make a lot of money—a poem
survives on just a few lines, with passion and style and
meter, if not rhythm, that most essential unessential tool
of life. You will not make money in poetry, or as
Thoreau put it, "No man is rich enough to keep a poet
in his pay."[20]

Of course, the person who plans to get rich stays clear of
book publishing altogether these days; it is the suicidal
poet who opens an independent bookstore, a small-
business person absolutely determined to probably not make

any money. Like a memo writer to
these leading nonmoneymakers
of America, Emily Dickinson writes,
"I dwell in possibility." This is
another way of saying, "I will
probably never go public,
but that's okay."

How to Handle One Particular Life Move— Marriage—So That You Don't Wake Up One Day and Suddenly Discover That You Are Rich

MARRY FOR love. That's all I'm talking about here. I have to mention it because in this day and age of prenuptial agreements, when not only the future and children but also fortunes are at stake, it is important to remember the following: *You could make money on your marriage.* Divorce is a tricky matter. With a good attorney, and some trumped-up psychological-harassment charges, you could be sitting pretty. So be certain to marry the person not because you like the sound of their parents' property, or because staying with him or her means half of the condo in Tampa, but because you are in love. This may sound like simple nonmoneymaking advice, but I know a divorce lawyer whose many cars and summer places say otherwise. And this is true for all kinds of marriages and partnerships. Love can be a crucial factor in not getting rich, because the one thing you can absolutely count on love for is to lead you on a path of distracting bliss, to a situation of unwealthy emotional strength, wherein you gaze out on the world of commerce and finance and shrug, safe in a meaningless cocoon of insolvent happiness, of devotion and allegiance made simultaneously more difficult and more meaningful in light of the constant onslaught of debt.

In general, love—love between a man and a woman or a woman and a woman or a man and a man or two friends or two relatives or any combination thereof—lands you in a small cove of peacefulness in the modern sea of untranquility, a cove that can mean everything to you but, if you put it on paper, isn't worth dink.

How *Not* to Not Get Rich

Among the basic types of people who can be said to be not rich are, first, the poor—who, if you laid out $9.95 for this book, are a group that most likely does not include you—and, second, those who are not rich and understand that they are not going to be rich and have either gracefully or grudgingly come to accept that and have, in lieu of a chalet in Colorado, decided to remodel the kitchen, or at least half of the kitchen—the second half is planned for next year. The third type of not-rich person is that person who wanted to be rich, who then was rich for a short period, and who now, through a series of incidents that might but would not necessarily include jail, injury, idiocy, disillusionment, procrastination, too much champagne, a television shopping network problem, or bad luck, has ended up no longer being rich and is *not* happy about it. This is the person who can be considered to have un-successfully unriched himself. A lot of the characters in Evelyn Waugh novels fall into this category, living on estates between the World Wars, eating on once beautiful but now chipped china, languishing in decay. But this category would also include someone like the celebrity real estate mogul Donald Trump, who, during the 1990s, accidentally got not so rich for a time, before eventually getting really rich again, his happiest state apparently. This group also includes countless formerly wealthy people who now live among us like us.

This group has presumably gotten not rich by accident, often in a manner that they are not happy with, often resulting in rash measures, such as jumping out of buildings, and the truth is I don't have a lot to say about that. My experience in not getting rich lies elsewhere. If you were once rich and are now not rich, then I must presume you either have a lot of natural not-getting-rich talent or none at all and your nontalent is momentarily dormant. If you are currently rich and you are interested in becoming not rich, then you will have to look elsewhere for advice. Just off the top of my head, I might recommend you read *The Grapes of Wrath* a few dozen times or take a vacation among the ever-dwindling middle class. But like I say, I don't want to give you bad how-not-to-get-rich advice.

How to Manage Your Time in General So That You Don't Wind Up a Billionaire or Anything Even Close to It

WASTING TIME, though last in this list of ways to not rake in the major buckaroos, is probably the most crucial ingredient to not getting rich—and yet people so often forget about it and wind up locked in their offices working for a boss who, ultimately, does not understand the value of time wasting, aka life. This is a shame since there are so many ways to waste time, besides reading a book about how not to get rich, including, just for example, letter writing. Nothing says "I'm screwing around and not becoming stinking rich" more than a letter to a friend: a letter filled with a sentiment that might sound cheap and

may even *be* cheap, but—by virtue of having been exe-
cuted with your pen in your hand, by virtue of you
yourself having unpeeled the self-adhesive postage
stamp—may have an intrinsic emotional value for the
person who receives it and reads it, thus wasting time on
the other end as well. Other excellent ways of wasting time
that will potentially have absolutely no impact on your
personal worth include fishing, quilting, calligraphy, wood
carving, digital photography, whittling, saddlemaking,
Ukrainian egg painting, the polka, watching TV, sand
art, storytelling, Bavarian beer-stein collecting, travel,
canasta, ham radio, computer gaming, pocket-watch repair,
macramé, snake collecting, boatbuilding, snowshoeing,
wooden duck decoy making, boccie ball, fantasy baseball,
sex, or any combination thereof.

Time-wasting possibilities are endless for people with
children. There are board games to play, model airplanes
to fly, and all kinds of things to talk about that will cause no
elevation of your personal financial picture whatsoever.
For instance, the benefits of reading to a child are twofold:
First, the parent is not making a lot of money, and, second,
as he or she reads to a young person, the parent is
establishing a valuable role model, setting the child up
for a life in which he or she may not be featured among
Forbes list of the wealthiest people in the world. Hanging
out with people who have retired at an early age and
without a huge stock portfolio is another great way to
waste time. But beware: How many times have we read of
the elderly miser, the man or woman who saved away
hundreds of thousands of dollars, who lived alone and
worked an unglamorous job and then bequeathed the
money upon his or her death to that neighbor who had
been kind, who had bothered to stop in and say hello? Well,
maybe we don't read about that kind of thing happening *too*

often, but the possibility that it might happen keeps some people who wouldn't otherwise be nice to elderly people being nice to elderly people, or at least I hope it does. That would be a neat little trick.

Wrapping Up on How Not to Get Rich— i.e., Concluding That Even If You Do Your Best, Something Might Go Wrong and You Could End Up Being Compared to a Rockefeller or Someone Even Richer

PLEASE UNDERSTAND. I'm not making any promises here. Not being rich is difficult, as we have seen, in this wealth-saturated day and age. You may end up being rich, you

may not. Because life itself is a gamble, let's face it. You
wake up in the morning, and you don't really know how it's
going to go. You could win the lottery and not even have
bought yourself a ticket—your wife slipped it into your
birthday card, or your best friend bought you one at lunch
because you looked as if you'd swallowed your razor at the
morning meeting when the boss had told your department
that it had better shape up. Or, on the other hand, this could
be the day that you get run down by a car, a really, really
fancy car driven by a movie star with an amazing lawyer.
"The so-called *victim*, Your Honor, was in fact the recip-
ient of an intimate encounter with Tad Brandolf that many
people would pay for, much less suffer a few minor broken
limbs . . ."

Some people are just naturally good at not getting rich.
They have a built-in wealth-prevention sense that guides
them along even in the most wealth-rich intersections of
their lives. They didn't buy Microsoft when a friend
mentioned that he was helping start up a new software
company. They sold their apartment in Manhattan for a
song in the seventies, instinctively believing the real estate
market would never, ever come back. It's as if these people
are being guided by an invisible hand, but not the invisible
hand that Adam Smith said drives capitalism to regulate
itself and moderate itself and generally cause the creation
of public wealth. It's the invisible hand of the guy in school
who, when you were growing up, was always pushing
people out the door of the gym, the door that locked from
the inside.

When you were locked out of the gym, you had little
choice except to walk around to the main school entrance
in your crappy school-issued T-shirt and gym shorts, the
winter chill on your legs and arms. There you were
greeted by the assistant principal, who assigned you

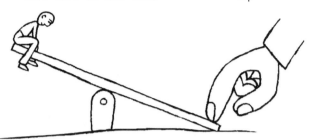

detention, basically the assistant principal's job, which, come to think of it, is not a bad one to look into as far as not getting rich goes. (You'd think assistant principals, of all people, would understand being locked outside, given that they are stuck being assistant principals, but they don't, of course, and so end up making things worse for you and no doubt for themselves).[21] Like being locked out of the gym, not getting rich is one of those situations where you can either panic or try to enjoy the walk back: the sun, the quiet, the chance to collect your thoughts as you walk practically naked through the school parking lot. In those few moments, though you have suffered a slight setback or misfortune—or what might be better described in this context as an *un*fortune—you are, if you think about it and don't get too tangled in the double negatives, not at that precise moment being *un*fortuned to any greater degree. You are in a holding pattern, as far as *un*fortune goes.

Maybe this sounds defeatist. Maybe it sounds worse. But it is merely recognizing that the accumulation of the wealth that surrounds virtual people in magazines is a wealth not meant for everyone—that the system that we call the economy works that way and doesn't mean it personally, despite what our Calvinist forefathers would say. People think it is their fault that they are not rich, or that they were pushed out the gym door on purpose. It's not. It's only their fault if they are a jerk about it. The fact is, the systematic nature of unrichness has been known to social scientists for decades,[22] and social safety nets were installed during the Great Depression to help individuals, which in turn helps everybody, and yet people still think the guy laid off down the street is a bum. People still think of themselves as bums.

The bottom line is, you're not a bum, even though being a bum is not necessarily a bad thing. And anyway, poverty does have its pluses, as perverse as that may sound. Paring down to the barest minimum essentials means you are no one's slave, that you have a lot less of a distance to fall should you run into real poorness, as in destitution. Especially in a society where we are bombarded with the teasings of luxury, less means more security. "The fact is, we are not a nation of homeowners," wrote Dorothy Day, the social activist, in 1953. "We are a nation of people owning debts and mortgages, and so enslaved by this installment buying that we do indeed live in poverty and precarity."

The line right next to the bottom is that you shouldn't feel like a bum, even if you are one, metaphorically speaking, or otherwise—and especially if you are in the long and complicated process of not getting rich.[23]

My hope is that if you follow the simple steps outlined herein, you will not get rich quickly and easily, and without the disappointment that so many people face when they go about things the other way—i.e., by not getting rich while trying hard to get rich. There might be changes in the economy, changes in the distribution of wealth through changes in the tax system, growth of unions that could once again increase the benefits of those who do not own corporations or at least own the corporations' shares. These might come through political changes or when the system is so lopsided that there isn't any more richness to redistribute to the already rich. There could even one day be a global situation that would be the financial equivalent of trying to get water from a stone.

In the meantime, waste as much time as you can while falling in love with someone or something beautiful or involving yourself in some nice combination. Keep reading and wasting time and keep your head down. With any luck, things will all work out all right.

Terms*

A good deal Something gotten, usually by someone other than you, at least in hindsight. For instance, let's say you yourself get a good deal; chances are that a more enlightened person will explain to you that what you thought was a good deal really wasn't very good at all. Thus the following sample exchange, the *I* being "you":

"I got a *good deal* on this."

"What did you get it for?"

"Four thousand dollars plus tax and delivery."

"Really? That seems a little high to me . . ."

Better than nothing This is a saying, and in some cases it is true, while in other cases it is not.

In the money Some scholars date the origin of this expression to the early pagan money festivals

* Or, things you might hear on the road to not getting rich.

of the Celts, wherein the god of riches, Buckus, was honored via the participation of an entire town or village in what we now know to be the first reality TV programs. As part of said ritual, the king would initially interview villagers seeking riches and, at the end of a typical six-week programming schedule, tar and feather one villager. Typically, the final program was heavily promoted by the network, even during the "news," and the winning villager was tarred and feathered in prime time. Other scholars disagree, and you can't blame them.

Left alone to his own devices A phrase that has nothing to do with either getting rich or not getting rich but that I nonetheless always enjoy hearing.

Short term When the credit card payment is due. Synonyms include *now, late, screwed,* and *yesterday.*

Long term A time that, like Zeno's paradox, continues to grow as you come closer to it; a place that is so far away that you might as well forget that it exists and concentrate on the short term, which, if you really think about it, is an easier way to get to the long term. From the Latin *innus yourus dreamuses.*

Spiritual wealth Wealth that is not actual. Not to be confused with *actual wealth.*

He'll get what's coming to him I, for one, sincerely hope not.

Poor as a church mouse Not really as poor as it might sound, in that the church mouse—aka the house mouse or *Mus musculus*—is relatively well-off in a church-type environment, generally speaking, assuming people are having coffee socials and teen pizza parties and the like. And anyway, mice experts tell us that, like most rodents, not to mention most mammals, mice are interested in the following, in no particular order: food, protection from predators, and mating—i.e., sex. (That's right, mice have sex in churches: let's see them try to ban *that* in a constitutional amendment.) If they've got most or even some of those, then they are, one can assume, content or "well-off" or "wealthy" or at least not poor. Antonym: *Poor as a human.*

Stinking rich A misnomer, in that you are not actually stinking. Synonyms include *filthy rich* as well as *filthy lucre*, of which Freud says things that I'd rather not repeat, if you don't mind. This is a family book about how not to get rich.

(Don't) Throw out the baby with the bathwater A popular expression.

You can take that to the bank Take *what* to the bank? That's what I want to know.

Hedge fund Come on—you don't believe that, do you?

Someday this is all going to pay off I'm not holding my breath.

Early to bed and early to rise, makes a man healthy, wealthy and wise Originally from Benjamin Franklin's *Poor Richard's Almanac*, Poor Richard being a misnomer as far as a pen name for Franklin goes. And by the way, don't you just

want to strangle Benjamin Franklin every time
you hear somebody say, "Early to bed and
early to rise, makes a man healthy, wealthy,
and wise"?

Waste not, want not See *Want not,
waste not.*

Want not, waste not See *Waste not,
want not.*

Want not, want not See your waiter.

Waste not, waste not I don't want to be
rude, but you ought to think about taking a little time off to
relax. Just for a couple of days.

Loaded Drunk.

Not a penny to his name A situation in which you have a
name but no money.

College fund A joke nowadays.

Savings account Give me a break!

Early retirement A make-believe land where fairy princesses
meet their true loves, and everyone lives happily ever
after.

Penthouse A house in which you feel cramped or pent up. As
in the following: "I've got to get out of this penthouse—it's
driving me crazy!"

Independently wealthy When you are on your own and think you don't have to worry about anyone else other than yourself. Examples include Enron.

More money than God That probably wouldn't be enough money either.

Rich Happy.

Happy Rich.

Appendix 1

THE FOLLOWING are the results of a survey taken in Great Britain in which workers in particular fields were asked whether they were happy or unhappy in their job. A psychologist interviewed by the newspaper reporting the findings said that blue-collar workers were more likely to get daily satisfaction in seeing a job well done, whereas white-collar jobholders didn't see the results of their work and were more likely to feel stress in a given day.

Hairdressers—40 percent happy
Clergy—24 percent
Chefs and cooks—23 percent
Beauticians—22 percent
Plumbers—20 percent
Mechanics—20 percent
Builders—20 percent
Electricians—18 percent
Florists—18 percent
Fitness instructors—18 percent
In-home health-care assistants—18 percent
Health-care professionals—17 percent

Media—16 percent
Chartered engineers—15 percent
Pharmacists—15 percent
Scientists—15 percent
Butchers—14 percent
DJs—13 percent
Interior designers—9 percent
Travel agents—9 percent
Teachers—8 percent
Bankers—8 percent
Accountants—7 percent
Information technology specialists—5 percent
Lawyers—5 percent
Secretaries—5 percent
Real estate agents—4 percent
Civil servants—3 percent
Architects—2 percent
Social workers—2 percent

Appendix 2

THE FOLLOWING is a list of people throughout history who were successfully not rich and not well known or not known at all.

Poorus of Miletus, ca. 612–582 B.C.
Flavius Brokavius, A.D. 68–110
Pope Anonymous, 1003–1043
Frederick the Mediocre, 1255–1302
Saint Peter of the Poorhouse, 1522–1568
El Fleghmo, 1575–1650
Pierre N'est pas Rien, 1680–1742
Adam Smithey, 1781–1822
Catherine the So-so, 1790–1855
George D'Annoy, 1886–1935
Myron Havaminute, 1920–1983
Edith Minnow, 1945–

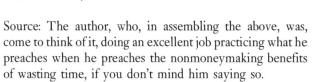

Source: The author, who, in assembling the above, was, come to think of it, doing an excellent job practicing what he preaches when he preaches the nonmoneymaking benefits of wasting time, if you don't mind him saying so.

Appendix 3

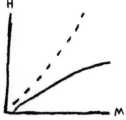

- - - The way you think it will be when you are not rich and hoping to get rich.

▬ The way it often really is.

H = Happiness
M = Money

Source: Just a feeling the author had after reading "The Real Truth About Money," by Gregg Easterbrook, in *Time*, January 17, 2005.

Notes

1. According to Amazon.com's "customers who bought this book also bought" heading, here is a comparison of the books also bought by purchasers of Dr. Phil's book and those bought by purchasers of Plato's complete works. The people who bought Dr. Phil's book also bought *The Ultimate Weight Solution: The 7 Keys to Weight Loss Freedom*, by Dr. Phil; *The Self Matters Companion: Helping You Create Your Life from the Inside Out*, by Dr. Phil; *The Life Strategies Workbook: Exercises and Self-Tests to Help You Change Your Life*, by Dr. Phil; *Relationship Rescue*, by Dr. Phil; and *The Ultimate Weight Solution Food Guide*, also by Dr. Phil. People who bought Plato's book also bought *The Basic Works of Aristotle*, by Aristotle; *The History: Herodotus by Herodotus*, by David Greene; *The Cambridge Companion to Plato*, edited by Richard Kraut; *Hellenistic Philosophy: Introductory Readings*, by Brad Inwood and L. P. Gerson; and *The Cambridge Companion to Aristotle*, edited by Jonathan Barnes. There were no overlaps—according to Amazon, no one who bought a Dr. Phil book also bought a book by Plato or any other ancient philosopher.

2. America has 2.2 million millionaires, according to an August 7, 2004, *Seattle Times* report by William Dietrich, entitled "From American Ethic to Global Imperative, the World of Work Turns." In an article in the London *Guardian* about a seminar on how to become a millionaire, I read the following statement by the seminar's host, Jon Riley: "Research shows that of the millionaires in the United States, eighty percent live well below their means. They are rarely employees, and they tend to live in the suburbs." I also read that millionaires like to hang out with other millionaires: "Millionaires say they like to meet with other millionaires and talk about money and financial matters. It's very important for them to swap skills." This makes good sense to me, in that, as a nonmillionaire, one of the things I try to do regularly is go to a bar in the city with my friend Dave, who, as far as I know, is also not a millionaire. There, we talk for a little bit about not being millionaires, while watching a ball game or chat with the bartender about someone or something that, chances are, has no financial relevance whatsoever. We engage in what might generously be considered nonskill swapping, which I enjoy and find relaxing.

3. Astoundingly, 8.2 million people are working and living in poverty, according to the AFL-CIO's economic research department. The federal government describes as poor an individual earning no more than $8,900 a year working for the minimum wage, or a family whose total income is less than $15,580. And yet, surveys show that most people view themselves, no matter how high or low their income, as middle class.

4. This is a joke stolen from the *Onion*, the satirical newspaper, which ran a news story headlined

"Four-Hundred-Dollar Stereo Put in $500 Car." My teenage son said this headline reminds him of our own car, which, even after 280,000 miles, is just fine, I don't care what you say.

5. Since 1980, as you may have noticed, real wages have dropped. Meanwhile, as you have probably heard by now, the average CEO pay during the same period rose 480 percent. (Not coincidentally, corporate profits rose 145 percent.) In 1980, CEO pay was 44 times the pay of the average worker. Today CEO pay is 301 times the pay of the average worker. Meanwhile, income for the top 1 percent of Americans climbed 157 percent, after adjusting for inflation. Adjusting for inflation is good to do in a situation like this because it takes your mind off the wide, wide discrepancy. I always adjust for inflation. In a world where someone makes 301 times more than you, I also adjust for humiliation and self-deprecation.

6. In "The Real Truth About Money," which appeared in *Time* on January 17, 2005, the writer Gregg Easterbrook, author of the book *The Progress Paradox*, cites a report by a University of Illinois psychologist who polled the members of Forbes 400, the wealthiest Americans. The psychologist discovered that the members were only a tiny bit happier than the rest of America. (The median American income, by the way, is approximately $43,000.) Other polls cited show that whatever their income level, most Americans feel they need more money to live well; that Americans who live modestly and anticipate better times ahead are happier than people

who live less modestly and are not expecting better times ahead; that the happiness poll numbers in America remain flat, even if America has gone from being a one-car nation to a two-car nation to an almost-three-car nation. "People tend to focus on the negative part and ignore the positive," Easterbrook writes. "Everyone needs a certain amount of money, but chasing money rather than meaning is a formula for discontent."

7. I read about Twain, who also said, "No money is the root of all evil," in *The Singular Mark Twain*, by Fred Kaplan.

8. According to *Time*, 90 percent of all Americans do not answer polling questions, even though, during elections and even during the rest of the time, it seems as if 90 percent of Americans listen to them. Then again, I noticed in a book that accompanied the U2 CD *How to Dismantle an Atomic Bomb* a statistic claiming that 65 percent of all statistics are made up on the spot, which shoots that poll that shoots polls in the foot in the foot.

9. Soros survived the Nazi occupation of Hungary, escaped to England, studied at the London School of Economics, founded and managed an international investment fund, and spends $400 million annually promoting freedom, open societies, public health, and economic reform. While you and I are reading this, he is also probably writing more books like the ones he has already written, such as *The Crisis of Global Capitalism: Open Society Endangered, Open Society: Reforming Global Capitalism*, and *The Bubble of American Supremacy: Correcting the Misuse of American Power.* If I ever woke up one day and found myself with an income that has, say, six or seven zeroes on it, I hope that I would end up

giving away at least $400 million annually. I should reiterate, however, that I see little chance of that ever happening, as should be obvious by now.

10. According to *An All-Consuming Century: Why Commercialism Won in Modern America*, by Gary Cross, the number of different items available in supermarkets has doubled approximately every ten years or so since the 1970s. I read this fact in *The Paradox of Choice: Why More Is Less*, by Barry Schwartz, a book that I thought about buying for a long time. I debated whether I needed a book that would tell me that I debated choices too much, but then I saw it for sale for only a dollar at my local library and just thought, *I'm going to go for it!*

11. People looking to get rich tend to think of suing someone as a good way to go about it. But as it turns out, not only is suing someone *not* a good way of getting rich, but not a lot of people sue—or at least not nearly as many as mainstream news stories and politicians suggest. There are stories in magazines and newspapers all the time about the "onslaught of litigation," as *Newsweek* put it. But in an excellent article entitled "The Myth of America's 'Lawsuit Crisis,'" Stephanie Mencimer, a contributing editor at *Washington Monthly*, pointed out that the number of people suing other people continues to drop. According to the National Center for State Courts, a research group funded by state courts, personal-injury and other tort filings, when population growth is factored in, have declined by 8 percent in the United States since 1975. In states where the population has grown dramatically in recent years, the drop has been even greater. In Texas, for example, tort filings fell by 37 percent between 1990 and 2000; and in California, they fell by 45 percent since 1994. Meanwhile, accord-

ing to the Justice Department, the median "jackpot" jury verdict in tort suits was only $37,000, which was down from $65,000 in 1992.

And yet stories about frivolous lawsuits keep popping up, their theme always being that the person made a lot of money easily. In 1977, according to Mencimer, an insurance company ran an ad describing a man who was awarded $500,000 when he was injured while using hedge clippers as a lawn mower; the ad agency subsequently admitted that the story was not based on fact. Other made-up stories that have nevertheless appeared in newspaper articles and on TV shows such as *60 Minutes* include one about the man who was awarded $300,000 after falling off a ladder because he set it in a pile of manure and sued the company for not telling him that the ladder should not be put in manure (the actual suit alleged that the ladder, advertised to hold 1,000 pounds, broke with 250 pounds on it); the woman who threw a soda at her boyfriend, slipped in the spilled drink, and sued the restaurant for $1,000 after breaking her tailbone (not true); the man who put his Winnebago on cruise control and went into the back while the Winnebago crashed and then successfully sued to have his Winnebago replaced (also not true); and the woman who climbed in a nightclub's restroom window, broke her front teeth in doing so, and was awarded $12,000 by a jury for dental expenses (not true as well).

The most famous suit that didn't go the way they like to tell you it did is the McDonald's coffee lawsuit. The headline in the *Wall Street Journal* on August 19, 1994, read, "Coffee Spill Burns Woman; Jury Awards $2.9 Million." The case was joked about on news programs and on late-night talk shows, and it has since become the urban-myth-like case that everyone points to when they talk about lawsuits being out of control. And yet, according to the *National Law Journal*, the result was completely justified. At the time, McDonald's sold its coffee at between 190 and 180 degrees, when 130 degrees is enough to cause third-degree burns. Between 1982 and 1990 there were seven hundred reports of severe burns from McDonald's coffee, many to young children and infants. McDonald's settled many of these suits out of court. The woman in the case that McDonald's lost was seventy-nine years old. She spilled the coffee while putting in milk and sugar and received third-degree burns that required reconstructive surgery and eight days in the hospital, which cost $11,000. She asked McDonald's to cover the cost; they offered $800. The McDonald's legal team would not settle with the woman's lawyer for $300,000 and would not pay the amount that a court-appointed mediator suggested, $225,000. The jury found that McDonald's had engaged in willful, reckless, malicious, or wanton conduct and awarded $2.7 million in punitive damages, based on the fact that McDonald's had $1.35 million in coffee sales daily at the time. The company later settled for a lower amount, but part of the agreement was that the amount would not be revealed.

The legal system is, quite obviously, not perfect, but it levels the playing field between people who are not rich and corporations that are very rich. Suing a lot is still not a good idea, but it is still a very good idea to have the ability to sue if you ever really have to.

12. Sea otters smash abalone shells on their chest using a small rock, and they tie themselves to the seafloor with kelp to sleep securely through the night, not that it

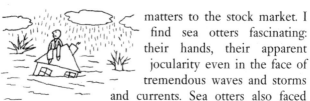

matters to the stock market. I find sea otters fascinating: their hands, their apparent jocularity even in the face of tremendous waves and storms and currents. Sea otters also faced great dangers from hunters who wanted their valuable coats; they were hunted so heavily in the eighteenth and nineteenth centuries that they had to be placed on the U.S. government endangered species list. Today, the populations have come back to a large extent, but conservationists would like to continue to protect them. Fishermen would like them off the endangered species list to protect the abalone harvest, but not me. I could watch a sea otter all day and not get bored—or rich, for that matter.

13. According the U.S. Department of Labor, two of the fastest-growing occupations between 2002 and 2012 are expected to be physician's assistants and network systems and data communications analysts. Both of these jobs require bachelor's degrees and both are expected to pay in the highest anticipated wage category, which is $41,820 and up. As bad luck would have it, many of the fastest-growing occupations that do not require college are also in the lowest-earning category. Home health aide is an example of the latter category, and the demand for home health aides is expected to grow by 50 percent. Other examples of jobs that will be in the highest demand in the lowest wage-earning category are maids and personal aides, categories that are expected to grow by 40 percent. The lowest expected earnings category is up to $19,600 a year—nobody seems to want to pay maids a lot of money.

14. A traditional joke regarding the moneymaking abilities
    of traditional musicians is as follows:

> Q: How do you make a million dollars as a
>   traditional musician?
>
> A: Start with two million.

I heard this joke at a traditional-music festival. I heard
it told by David Jones, an exquisite singer of old folk
songs, ballads, and sea shanties, who sings
regularly at the South Street
Seaport in New York City,
and at various folk festivals
along the East Coast.

   As far as I know, David
Jones is not raking it in
singing folk songs. I should
also note, with reference to the idea of
mandolin players owning a yacht, that the late Johnny
Carson, who was a drummer, once asked, rhetorically,
"Is that the banjo player's Porsche?"

15. In not investing in stocks you will be in excellent
    company, as nearly 40 percent of the nation is stock-
    free. That's 100 million people, or twelve and one half
    times the population of New York City.

16. In 2004, total household debt was $9 trillion, a figure
    that has grown by more than 50 percent over the past
    five years, according to the Federal Reserve Bank of
    St. Louis.

17. Jefferson invented a number of items for use around
    the farm, which is where he hoped everyone would be
    working, including a plow and a clock that showed the
    hour and the day of the week. He surrounded himself
    with a kind of homemade classical luxury, but at the
    same time he was homespun: Jefferson insulted the
    British ambassador when as president he showed up to

greet him wearing house slippers. According to *Thomas Jefferson: A Life*, by Willard Sterne Randall, Jefferson also wrote, "The sentiments of men are known, not only by what they receive, but what they reject also."

18. Sometimes attempting to grow your company and reap commensurate profits can be another way to not get rich, as the Vlasic pickle company famously showed. In the 1990s, Vlasic was selling its pickles to Wal-Mart. At one point, Wal-Mart asked Vlasic to make a gallon-sized pickle jar that would be sold for a little under $3—a bottle of pickles that might be displayed at an agricultural fair, the kind of event that, incidentally, would be held on an old fair ground, the very type of ground that a megastore not unlike Wal-Mart would choose to build on these days. Vlasic concentrated on Wal-Mart's request to the detriment of its other business. Soon, they were having trouble finding enough pickles, and so many people bought so many Vlasic pickles at Wal-Mart that Vlasic lost business elsewhere—people reached what might be called their natural pickle-buying limit. Vlasic eventually went into bankruptcy, though company executives (amazingly) argued that the Wal-Mart pickle problem was not a factor. Many other smaller companies fail under the strain of their success with Wal-Mart, according to an article in the December 2003 issue of *Fast Company* by Charles Fishman. Thus, we see that growing your small company into something too big can also be a way to ultimately stay not

loaded—a fact that I wish more companies would rec-
ognize, not that many companies listen to me. On the
other hand, one can't just thank Wal-Mart for not getting
us all rich. In a February 2005 op-ed piece in the *New York
Times*, Robert Reich, the former labor secretary, wrote,
"The fact is, today's economy offers us a Faustian
bargain: it can give consumers deals largely because it
hammers workers and communities. We can blame big
companies but we're mostly making this bargain with
ourselves. The easier it is for us to get great deals, the
stronger the downward pressure on wages and benefits.
Last year, the real wages of hourly workers, who make up
about 80 percent of the work force, actually dropped for
the first time in more than a decade; hourly workers'
health and pension benefits are in free fall." Reich
proposes a requirement that companies with more than
fifty employees offer health insurance to their employees. "My inner consumer won't like that very much, but
the worker in me thinks it a fair price to pay."

19. David Bunn is an artist and a poet who uses discarded
cards from the card catalogs of libraries to create art—
an area of expertise that, I would bet, no millionaire
would recommend for aspiring millionaires. He began
when he found the Los Angeles library's discarded
catalog cards in 1990. He subsequently began to
present the cards—chosen and arranged in order
and framed and mounted—as found poetry. He has
worked with other card catalogs, such as that from
Liverpool, England. Here is an example of a poem that
is a list of exact titles in the order they appeared in a
card catalog:

Show me!
show me

show me a hero
show me a land
show me a miracle
show me how to write (in manuscript)
show me Japan
"show me" Missouri
show me the good parts
show me the way
show me the way to go home
show me the way to go home
show me the world of space travel
show me where the good times are

So how did Bunn become a self-taught card-catalog poet/artist? Did he read about it as a career choice in a self-help book? No. According to an interview with him in the November 2000 issue of *Art in America*, entitled "Relics of the Material Age: David Bunn Turns Library Catalogue into Poetry," by Leah Ollman, Bunn credits his liberal arts degree for his success as card-catalog poet/artist. "I think one of the wonderful things about a liberal arts college is that you can explore what it means to be a human and be critical and be aware and you don't have to know where you're going to settle as much as you learn how to risk things," he said.

20. Not that it matters, really, but the author would just like to say that in his own richest time-wasting modes, he imagines a world in which the great poets are the CEOs. He sees futures traded, in other words, not only on coffee and copper and hogs but on beauty and sadness and happiness as well. He sees Gerard Manley Hopkins creating huge sonnet factories. He sees Robert Frost outsourcing

heroic-couplet manufacturing overseas, while keeping some heroic-couplet manufacturing going here in the United States, which makes everyone happy, even though many people are not certain what a heroic couplet is. A heroic couplet, as the reader may well be aware, is a rhyming pair of lines that is usually in iambic pentameter but can also be in tetrameter, and the rhyme scheme, generally speaking, is *aabbcc* and so on. The form was often used for the translation of classical epic poetry. Here is an example of heroic couplets, as seen in an Anne Bradstreet (ca. 1612–72) poem entitled "The Author to Her Book":

Thou ill-form'd offspring of my feeble brain,
Who after birth did'st by my side remain,
Till snatcht from thenceby friends, less wise than true,
Who thee abroad expos'd to public view,
Made thee in rags, halting to th' press to trudge,
Where errors were not lessened (all may judge).
At thy return my blushing was not small,
My rambling brat (in print) should mother call.
I cast thee by as one unfit for light,
Thy Visage was so irksome in my sight,
Yet being mine own, at length affection would
Thy blemishes amend, if so I could.
I wash'd thy face, but more defects I saw,
And rubbing off a spot, still made a flaw.
I stretcht thy joints to make thee even feet,
Yet still thou run'st more hobbling than is meet.
In better dress to trim thee was my mind,
But nought save home-spun Cloth, i' th' house I find.
In this array, 'mongst Vulgars mayst thou roam.
In Critics' hands, beware thou dost not come,

And take thy way where yet thou art not known.
If for thy Father askt, say, thou hadst none;
And for thy Mother, she alas is poor,
Which caus'd her thus to send thee out of door.

The author of the very book you are holding even sees Yeats chairing a meeting on symbolism in the marketplace while wearing a microphone headset, à la Madonna or even Britney Spears, while prancing around onstage in his great Victorian cape like one of those guys in the infomercials. And then there's Emily Dickinson, the seer of beauty, allocating billions into research for rhymes with the word *orange* and still never coming out of her office, always sending out cryptic messages, short little e-mails full of hyphens and a profound sense of sadness that makes every employee pause at his or her delete button.

21. Carlos Cipolla, an Italian economist and a historian of technology who taught in Italy and at the University of California at Berkeley, was also the author of a short treatise entitled *The Basic Laws of Human Stupidity*. Cipolla's *Laws* was a best seller in Europe and made into a popular play in Italy. The so-called Third Basic Law of Human Stupidity applies in the instance of the assistant principal giving you detention even though you were shoved out the door of the gym and locked out by someone other than yourself. The third law is this: "A stupid person is a person who causes losses to another person or to a group of persons while himself deriving no gain and even possibly incurring losses."

22. If you take the train to Milwaukee, instead of flying or driving there, and you get off at the Amtrak station and

walk toward the downtown area where the hotels and incredible breweries and sausage places are, you pass a little park called the Wisconsin Workers Memorial. The park features a sculpture that is also a time line noting the years 1911, when Wisconsin enacted the nation's first workers' compensation law, and 1920, when Wisconsin drafted the first unemployment compensation law; a quote on a plaque taken from a book called *The Rise of Labor and Wisconsin's Little New Deal* says, "The 19th Century belief that unemployment was a matter of individual bad luck or bad character was deeply ingrained in Wisconsin and American culture, and the realization that in fact it was an unavoidable feature of the modern industrial economy came only slowly."

23. A song I love about being a bum was first sung in the beginning of the 1900s by hoboes and Wobblies, Wobblies being members of the IWW, or Industrial Workers of the World. It is called "Hallelujah, I'm a Bum." For a long time people thought it was just a folk song, not necessarily written by one person or another. Carl Sandburg had it in his song collection, *The American Songbag.* Sandburg, who bummed around as a hobo for a while, wrote this about it: "This old song heard at the water tanks of railroads in Kansas in 1897 and from harvest hands who worked in the wheat fields of Pawnee County, was picked up later by the I. W. W., who made verses of their own for it, and gave it a wide fame." Harry McClintock, an old Wobbly songwriter, has claimed authorship, saying he put new words to an old song, "Revive Us Again." A good place to hear "Hallelujah, I'm a Bum" is on a CD called *Parades & Panoramas*, a collection of songs from *The American*

Songbag, by Dan Zanes, a guy I know who may or may not have been hoping to get rich by recording old folk songs, I'm not sure. The lyrics, which can of course vary wildly, are as follows:

> *Verses* (and feel free to make up your own):
> Why don't you work
> Like other folks do?
> How the hell can I work
> When there's no work to do?
>
> Oh, why don't you save
> All the money you earn?
> If I didn't eat, I'd
> have money to burn.
>
> Oh, I love my boss,
> And my boss loves me,
> And that is the reason
> I'm so hungry.
>
> *Chorus:*
> Hallelujah, I'm a bum
> Hallelujah, bum again,
> Hallelujah, give us a handout
> To revive us again.

If you are like me—and let's hope you're not—when you sing it, you feel kind of free.

Your Notes on How Not to Get Rich